C000165141

Melt & Solve

RODDY LUMSDEN (born 1966) is a Scottish poet, who was born in St Andrews. He has published five collections of poetry, a number of chapbooks and a collection of trivia, as well as editing a generational anthology of British and Irish poets of the 1990s and 2000s, *Identity Parade*. He lives in London where he teaches for The Poetry School.

ALSO BY RODDY LUMSDEN

BOOKS
Yeah, Yeah, Yeah (1997)
The Book of Love (2000)
Roddy Lumsden is Dead (2003)
Mischief Night: New & Selected Poems (2004)
Third Wish Wasted (2009)
Terrific Melancholy (2011)
The Bells of Hope (2012)
Not All Honey (2014)

PAMPHLETS
Super Try Again (2007)

ANTHOLOGIES
Identity Parade: new British and Irish poets (2010)
The Best British Poetry 2011 (2011)
The Salt Book of Younger Poets, with Eloise
Stonborough (2011)

Melt & Solve

by

Roddy Lumsden

SALT

CROMER

PUBLISHED BY SALT PUBLISHING
12 Norwich Road, Cromer, Norfolk NR27 0AX, United Kingdom

© Roddy Lumsden, 2015

First published by Salt Publishing 2015

Printed in Great Britain by Clays Ltd, St Ives plc

Typeset in Paperback 9 / 13

ISBN 978 1 78463 042 3 paperback

1 3 5 7 9 8 6 4 2

For Heidi Seppälä, minun sairaanhoitajani,
mainio tanssija, rakastettu tytär

Contents

Author's Note

In the early hours of 1st September 2013, I had an accident. Not sure what happened, but it seems I sleepwalked out of bed, something I am prone to doing, and slipped on some books and magazines which were by my bed. I hit my head against the wall very hard. I recall only a few seconds, 'ouch that hurt', then I fell unconscious and did not wake until the next evening.

'How long does concussion last?' I asked the doctor who checked me out. 'How long is a piece of string?' she replied. I thought concussion was a couple of groggy hours after a bang on the head. But if you hit hard, concussion can last months, years even. It is a dispiriting condition. Parts of your brain are working normally, other parts are spinning, misfiring. My balance was awful, I forgot little things like needing to buy a train ticket; anything organisational became twice as hard. I misted over when it came to anything to do with forms, numbers, email and so on.

I was not myself. I found myself one evening in the wrong part of London, having taken a wrong train. I sat on a wall in Ladywell and cried. It took me an hour to recalibrate, sort myself and find home. I remembered who I had been but became increasingly aware that I did not feel like I was that person. I started slowly to impersonate the person I had been. I learned his lines.

But my creativity had gone with the head injury. Bad thing for a writer. I had written next to nothing in the months after the accident. In the first few hours of 2014, I was talking with my poet friend Camellia Stafford. Always a good late talker. The next day, I wrote a poem about our conversation. I decided to use lower case, no punctuation save for one decisive colon, four couplets. I wanted to start to write again.

Writing would help me refind myself. This is where this book began.

And this is where the restrictions began. Rules would help me back into being productive. I had my form. My rules were these: whenever I had an interesting late night conversation, I would write a poem about it; whenever I was near the Thames, I would write one then; whenever I was on Tranquil Vale, the main street where I live in Blackheath and it was raining I would have to write one; whenever I was feeling particularly concussed, I would force myself to write about that.

Inevitably, the poems were at times disjointed, offbeat. The first third of this book is, I agree, odd (stick with it – it gets easier!). My brain was odd. I was also interested in the compositional process of a favourite contemporary US poet, Noelle Kocot, who talks of 'brewing' poems. The work happens before the writing, rather than in the rewriting. You brew, chew, then write and leave it as it is. Nothing in this book has been revised. I thought I would write fifty of these little poems, but became re-enamoured with a favourite film, Peter Greenaway's *Drowning By Numbers*, a film which has an obsession with the number 100. With a mixture of excitement and resigned alarm, I knew I had to write another fifty.

On the wall of The Pineapple pub in Lambeth, where I have a drink with my students after classes, there is a reproduction of a painting, *A Special Pleader* by Charles Burton Barber, a Victorian painter who fancied himself as the new Turner, but who had continued success with sentimental paintings mainly featuring small girls and dogs. He disliked doing this but needed the money. Another artist is important to the sequence, Henry Darger, a Chicagoan artist and writer who wrote a 15,000 page novel and constructed numerous unusual artworks which were fed by his obsessions.

The series of plaintive poems entertains the idea of sentimentality. It encourages fetishes, by which I mean repeated references and name dropping. It is 'hand on heart' stuff. Sweeping, indulgent last lines, often. Emotional, evoking the mood I found myself in as I recovered, solved.

RODDY LUMSDEN

N.I.T.A.

And with calm-planted steps walk'd in austere;
'Twas Apollonius: something too he laugh'd,
As though some knotty problem, that had daft
His patient thought, had now begun to thaw,
And solve and melt: - 'twas just as he foresaw.

JOHN KEATS, 'Lamia'

'What are you doing up so late?'
'I'm counting the stars.'
'You really know all their names?'
'Yes, I do.'
'How many did you count?'
'A hundred.'
'There are more than a hundred.'
'I know.'
'Why did you stop?'
'A hundred is enough. Once you have counted a hundred, all
the other hundreds are the same.'

opening scene from Peter Greenaway's *Drowning By Numbers*

late night conversation (camellia)

chaise longue for you then ouch I take
the new year stance in my place of guilt

which of the base emotions did then we
select to marketeer and gracelessly suss

the guddleable heart rises to the riverscape
of our soft talk and our guesswork

i will as ever tell you all and you to me
though daylight heists it: I recall you kind of

long term concussion in midwinter (midlife)

hoping I would be the one to luck up
and turn that tough kid card the mistigris

hope or seldom home: seldom being a cottage
under blaze of gauze or a blurt of drizzle

enriched enough just for the hardstare
and my precarious whack of poker chips

a beetle buffed table where we would deal
and bluff as storm rocked the yawing shed

rain on tranquil vale (rem sleep)

these candles in the railway: offside
props in my cancelled erotic film

the slack skin of the honey badger means
he will only ever lose one fight

having sought the exact I know now
only this haze and the next excess

the honeyguide does not dream but
she leaks idea and sees the tree tide flip

late night conversation (brian)

that his sentient wives nixed henry since
his joust wound never healed and wept

that new orleans rasps and rainsticks: a rum do
as it tilters congaing into the gulf

that henry met anne only a lancethrow from
where we now speak and his face fell at hers

that we lie in our beds as holbein lied with paint
and the blues and the fall and the fall and the blues

the thames at limehouse ($\therefore$ wide)

impressions of each other then these impressions
of each other being squeal stomp shrug

the rainswept and the freezeswept balcony
hears secrets which will coat and cloak

the river breathes as air simplifies it
which is all we need in our pretendings

all rivers breathe: if midnight rises
my microsaccades will pepper you again

late night conversation (frith)

as when the room does not flick to grey
and some one has died but it is not us

zantzinger still swings his dandy toy
in an age which did and could not contain us

now I am valuing your brow and your value
for like dylan I vowed to dig the rational

if I could see my face in this table or anywhere
I can but would not sing it: I do not walk that chain

[8]

long term concussion in midwinter (midori)

much fear simplifies as hot denial of fear
of the self and lo the traffic grims on

all been in the mood to lie grim and to grim
with all grim watercolouring our thought

say some thing pretty the skull will tell
my bellyish brain: I think of devon or petting

there are sorts who cluck at the sight of a melon
or sit on the back step and only smell bacon

[9]

the thames at wapping (∴ fast)

thirteen days and a beard will soften
and retain weather and the shrapnel scent of tuna

swift water is so soft you would throw you
into it as into a bespoke chamber of cushions

lights treble and swivel for the sweet hearts
promenading though clear there are none

winter: lights trade and how forlorn to know
and need its songs but long to never hear them

rain on tranquil vale (retread)

box office poison: a star whose hype got hoisted
and hiked but ruined the takings of the fleapits

it never yet spoiled us so we are welcome not
to reinvent or replay our few replay games

at least we are not man down or woman overboard
and the sea stares flat and nobody treading

none of us are what they called the triple threat
meaning one who could act and sing and tread

rain on tranquil vale (retro)

thinking of being bunked out and the cottage:
one i would have bought had life done different

and then kasenetz katz and an understanding
i will never be a hazelnut swirl for anyone

a wish i could dive into that sugar shoppe
and a knowing i am hard tack and seggs

things coming at me through bastard snow
are not snapping wolves but they are not love

rain on tranquil vale (regarding raina)

i lift a tin to what i thought our one night
which was dishy until it skewed and huffed

five hours on my lap and you being these:
gishy and corvine and cordite and oh

then you called some names i did not need
and all for such little scuttle and bust

as if i did not have names for my own unease
growing as vines do round my pantry door

long term concussion in midwinter (mid evening)

the finnish dancers would not butter their okra
and will not spice their green lentils

the wild legumey and pulsy scent sprinks
our cage as i heat a cheapskate pollock pie

i listen to fractions rather louder than i can bear:
music calms but it butts my bearish head

then fractions again and then fractions again
and then whatever is behind that hard pulled curtain

late night conversation (josh)

the polygraph is grapeseed stuff and
the gangsters chew their cheeks to cheat it

but you say it dints the passion killers
who suffer the rubdown of the one off blast

we weaken: by which i mean the lieutenant parts
of all that i have been avoiding in my saying

by which i mean my all time mission which
if i had a mission I could call my mission

long term concussion in midwinter (midshipman)

if i am of this person or of this region why
do i have my alice as we all seem to do

also a weary heifer who kinks as she goes
into the gang funk that makes the steak

not that i am mixing my ideals: more
that i know i have been treated dirtily

yes and try to think of living on a skiff where
these lessons are many filthy miles askance

long term concussion in midwinter (midden)

the grimy venus of cranach or the long slink
of a glacier: ouch i am done folks

bucket of my own filth or a yikes
sidling at whatever miles per hour

in the pile they found signs of the most
serious signs of life and also of glass

glass as if smart stuff yes as if it does not
cover the most part of the old kent road

rain on tranquil vale (redouble)

as if the kneel and fall were not the thing
and i was polar explorer and not bad diamond

and the spin stopped and i saw my non doppel
not in the quicksand and not in the eddy

which pole to visit: the one where your songs
are playing and your waxing crush shy smiles

i never whistle and never stroll and know
such niceties occur for those not at my brink

long term concussion in midwinter (midst)

since thinking we were closer than now i see
we were i now mistrust each supping face

here in a horseshoe bar where my relevance clings
one handed and i yank and ratchet the pinion

unhoist: i summon oughtred and napier
and want their gentlemanly calibrations

now i summon thomas alva edison
with his halo of overrated fizz

late night conversation (roddy)

you to me said leaping dolphin tattoo is worst
or auspicious work of art or any piety

the boy in the railway has clowny eyes
and is sad or stoned and becomes your shrug

empty people and um quoting from pocahontas
whose journey was more gif than glyph

my awful: to on a back road meet her on
a tattoo pony beating a tattoo and showing ink

long term concussion in midwinter (middling)

if i am on the versus or the very ouch
and have already said then sorry salutations

if then the future brings you to my thought
well look up railways short and high and bright

check for the barmaid who just called me darling
and looks like my lover who died young

investigate: the sweet parcel from nowhere oh
and styled silence measured by tick of clock

late night conversation (dominic)

we can talk discomfort of primes for long as you like
for the mood has gone to primes and here we are

an us divisible by two and ever the chalk and cheese
that makes our friendship say computable

seventeen times fifty nine could be that day
i was first kissed or nineteen nineteens the end of it

music of the primes you say: though some one dreaming
scheherazade and some one leagues under the sea

long term concussion in midwinter (midas)

only now that they are tandem eating i
am sure these bonbon girls are twins

that more fetching romulus my doppel
is out there naming things by deathly hindsight

he names solferino and names the dromedary
then names the dewberry and some far isle

all i touch to name is doomed and i am here: my
both hands clamped to the scuppered scalp

late night conversation (heidi)

the downdog brisk of taupin americana:
buttermilk bristling on some scorched porch

cowboyish thoughts of the wilded heat
in places you and i will never stride

men who stroll from chapel to church
are not to be trusted and not to be texted

there is what we understand and ouch what
we half and quarter and eighth understand

late night conversation (frith)

if ever you could source a policy you should
for i reckon to the way a heart cascades

it is direction down and some come hither to lovers
and some we hear risk double spouse

and those few who cross a bridge between persuasions
hauling their bloomers or breeches as they scuttle

we switch and those who know we switch
switch head alongways such as this: now switch

late night conversation (lee)

the beard is on its lazy journey down the face
or lazy is moving down our slug slow redemption

sea captains and prophets of the older testament
and all the jihad giddies all agree the chin

some women wow and their senses wow even
while others sick in corners crying no to that

hush: what can be my parameters on beards
or any thing if my parameters are quarantined

long term concussion in spring (estimate)

wasps are what i want and beetles scuffing and
hockey girls are what i want and proper heart music

and the land where my deal roosts ugh
is what i want and you who knows me true

or not to hear the blather oh the especial blether
of: here we call it the only place to be

been measured and been there with a ruler
on my billy or a doctor saying five foot nine

long term concussion in spring (estate)

the tidying is not me and the breasts of gemma
not me and the idea of ireland is not me

the risk of blame is not: not now or the risk
of too much brotherhood or sisterhood

thank you for the dizzy which is not much me
or the needy leaning or the late night wail

there is a place i live or some would say
abide or some would fool faced say reside

long term concussion in spring (establishing)

numbmindingly thumbing my love scars
from the best of all kittens ever

now i scope the feast we would prosper
if we did find the fear to marry

our friend has no advice: instead says
i would get wankered at that wedding

oh the bem casados and the gamopilafo
and oh the magistery of the tang yuan

long term concussion in spring (escalation)

when i yanged my skull my inner sophisticate
bit down on some found thing and fled

because i play for the score and not
for the win i am a champion sort still

i suggest if the evening now is nicing
it is such as the day was a day made of thick

best is the sound of a child counting: a child
counting its sweet intrinsic increment

late night conversation (fred)

finding a light switch in the gloom as if
finding a lobster blistery from the depth

it is as big as the land speed car bluebird
and its fists like the arms of sonny liston

now i am on the misty lit night terrace
at doxford hall: all has turned greenaway

far london falls simple and all silence brims
with mozart mozart slim harpo emmylou

rain on tranquil vale (revalue)

now the sugariest apple is a bartlett pear
and the oak a shrub and mist is ocean

now the neat shamrock belts into bush
or the eland tends its marsupial instinct

rutland twists to riga and my imperial hush
must dip as I will not have these limits

decades skip and i wade this slant puddle:
a weimaraner can coast through a mousehole

late night conversation (pat)

beware: the english have their systems and irish
must commingle in necessary huck and drear

man must persist or else it breaks dawn
and dawn is when the weakened die off best

no one pulled a steady draught and thought
a thirsty man would not appear to his work

no one staged a show trial and made belief
a mouse would snoot sweet across that scene

rain on tranquil vale (rerun)

valid or solve: some talk of anarchy yet and
i saw a small boy fall halfway through his race

he chuckled when he spilled and sent clear
that it was better than winning and i concur

tonight i hauled out the first name of degas
and spoke too loudly of the life of darger

all this life i have tried to turn the cameo
into something more and have run and run run

long term concussion in spring (especial)

all sliding out like easy lambs or nail scissors:
the gush they use to deal with forest fire

and the lip of night or the taunt of night
and me shunting to the lips of sleep

the way perfection scares or the dread lovely
of the absolute: do not question me at this point

i have sleep sort of on my side and i do not
want questioning since you have to trust me

rain on tranquil vale (res gestae)

how can i stamp on the snails on the terrace
with me not having the brigand tendency or touch

a wrong turn lucked princip to the killing
of franz ferdinand and i was not there

the most must thing is me not thinking bella
or her this or her that or her supple consonants

i want to continue mostly as nature intended:
the abstract dimmed to a faint peep or a skew

long term concussion in spring (estrange)

hold me people and hold me becky and hold me
triceratops which stands to the edge of my fear

hold me mother and hold me charlie and joan
of arc was not burned: do not believe that myth

shall we talk about the head and how it is
in so many ways us and that we are burned

i diff back from the balcony and imagine
all your sneers and all i think is hold me bella

long term concussion in spring (esurient)

the night not quiet and me writing: may
you dream of the sweetest of hazelnuts

geier hugs me on the terrace and claims
he will not give up the world of shipping

a hug from a man is fine with me if it is right
and sweet if the world swings afterwards

i aim to be better and it is right that i heart thump
and namtap sleeps perfect in chaotic nightwear

rain on tranquil vale (recidivism)

fleetwood mac is fine with me and the rain
and trees are asking me for terrorous lies

honey you know who you are: your ganging lies
are calling you to me from unsubtle distance

pfft pftt you would say when crossbowing
or pistoling some enemy in your edge of sleep

i will say trigger if you say demolition
though time and cameras are our best of judges

rain on tranquil vale (reggae)

let us greek this up a little: the rain tonight
is lucid but ugh it is also peeni walli

i contemplate if the bulgy girl who caused
the accident in that song is still with us

i know so little about those trojans
but am close to being willing to learn

so unconscious, did not know what to do
sings the man as troy drifts from land to land

late night conversation (jesus and the crusader)

we must sort ourselves and start tomorrow
says the crusader and we stand in the rain

ocd and mania and paranoia: how screwed
are we boys outside the inn of ancient heritage

wat tyler and anne of cleves ran their gas
across this heath and now we gawk at the dark

we must is one thing but ancient is exaggeration
so i apologise but not enough to learn saxophone

rain on tranquil vale (reward)

manic and my back hard to the wall
and rainy night in soho playing

i wonder if when i think of you thus
you sense it across the boroughs

my mother used to take me to see the fox
kept penned at the local slaughterhouse

i have known thus: i have known you
and some would think that the best of plenty

long term concussion in early summer (sucre)

what are you doing here lautrec and whingey
with your talk of boats you have not liked

the ruckus of the music I have privileged:
afraid not just of the night but all of it

cocaine is not for me and london drags
my lungs and heels for better dances

i lived across a century end and did not feel
i had to bow and bow out when it gulped

long term concussion in early summer (suture)

hold me kim and hold me cheryl and hold me
all of you as i swoop through this issue

you may need to stitch me or catch the fall
though some times i feel that we are us:

i feel tori doing pele or feel sydney at zennor
having had a sniff of more than the black light

ouch only stitches grip me so hold me daisy
hold me ruby hold me ninette hold me rubella

long term concussion in midsummer (midsummer)

as we sort a walk tomorrow raina writes do not
call it raina time for reasons we need not plough

a week since our last walk and the talk of a bad
hand dealt and being both outside and looking in

i offer instead my arrangement with her: a woman
of character and she replies a woman of disorder

mozart stood on a bridge and bliss would resolve
and form in his perfect but same time smutty ears

the thames at westminster bridge (∴ jittering)

if the river snags the last hooks of my giddy
then be it that i can allow this lilac sky

marker and beacon and jetty performing far
from where they clean my stain from that wall

my headswell welcomes an essence of sentiment
dripped from a bottle as dark as this water below

now one liquid line is hauled towards another
at some embracing coast or coaxed up segue: solve

By Numbers

I wasn't
myself, as they say. Or I was myself utterly,
for the first time.

MARIANNE BORUCH, 'After Surgery'

Oh dearie me, I'm in a state.
Oh and what will I do when salvation comes?
What do you think?
I've had such a good time, honest,
in your squalid and wobbly world.

Microdisney, '464'

Plaintive 1

They asked me, 'what do you think of
the smell of money, the smell of a woman
and the smell of the sea?' I held firm.
Night wavered and people were singing.
The smell of the sea I know, I said,
but I am not an informer. The smell
of a woman is my purposeful business
and you and I are damned on that.
The smell of money though, you have me on:
it has taken my heart. It has taken my life.

Plaintive 2

Supposing the thing I wished was night
was wrong, what did I learn? Efficacy,
yes and then the night became the night
and just the night. Roaming, tiredness,
human weakness. I tilted, being person,
and able to construct or confuse. Trees
were swilling. I believed I knew my depths.
Robes, no. I thought dark, strangled robes
then not dark, not strangled, not robes,
Then think about it, then solve yourself.

Plaintive 3

How every thing is tomorrow. The spoon
with its sweet face is saying tomorrow.
The cream wall is glancing. You can guess.
Or the urge. Or the threat of simplicity.
Some times people sing to themselves.
That is that. And that they go to the fridge
and summon miracles which are not so,
but their lives continue. Lives putter
into grit, or shine, or dab. I have been.
Say one thing *that* of me, that I have been.

Plaintive 4

For example, a girl in a black dress, last night,
and the song about the little nut tree came
buzzing. And then the fly, I knew, dizzying
on its slippy branch. And solace, which
I hear exists. So my whatever psyche
said forget the fly, erase. But, its black wings
and its solemn roar and its flexy hooks
and how brisk the tree buds come and how
quick I don't. Then the soapy, flipside shame
of the sudden. And a dread of that jet black.

Plaintive 5

Oh, animal Holborn drifting in smirr,
the people tell me there are ten sure things
of which I know just two – that rain
will some times sing and the other has
sudden escaped me. But a night drags fear in.
Hold me Heidi. Hold me Lucy. Hold me
Amy. Hold me nieces. Hold me Rosie.
The rainy scattering. Those fine old songs.
Blur of it. Zoo of it. Bad carnival mind.
Lonesome, ship, down. Hold me Bella.

Plaintive 6

The sound of someone walking with a crutch
is something you know and also the sound
of a sea captain clutching to his last horse.
A great sniff from a hundred yards off
can wake you from the loneliest of sleeps.
What shall I bring to this table? Drums
or hard bit finesse. And the very most idea
of a table. I stir. Then I pestle and I mortar.
You *must* believe me. What good walking
out of these woods if you will not believe?

Plaintive 7

A feline asking. Or my latest poor drawing
of a cat. Or small girls and their impressions
of lions, thousands of them, worldwide wide
and down the years. Cat night and cat song.
A young tom skirting the stream which lazies
through the Lade Braes, where once I settled
the sweet face of a speedwell close to my own.
Ask is all. Ask is a chill lull at the wood's edge.
Now I know you ask the lord until you learn
to ask for love. Until that wood sits with you.

Plaintive 8

George, the sad, sweet uncle who died
before my age never heard 'Big My Secret'
or 'Children on the Hill'. Asthma and, and
the constant cigarettes. Nyman pushes his plate
and Budd flicks off the radio. Rope unswivels
and the world wakes. I need my business.
He loved the greats and I do not trust the greats.
To trust is to open yourself. See my flicks.
Gone soon. My game uncle who was who, what?
Dividend of sadness added to the chime.

Plaintive 9

Not El Greco as a painter, but El Greco
as an idea, as a cove drifting the woods
for dark taints. And not as a man to drink with
or reach to, but perhaps for a discussion
of mariolatry or porcelain. Perhaps for decency,
its fundament, what I might nightly strive to.
And sentiment, that milky Victorian thing,
with its silly give, with its century lull;
my hand on my chest, my stupidest hand
on my stupidest heart. My best of captures.

Plaintive 10

Intro. When you stole me the pomegranate
or gave me the acorn which I by time thought
too precious to plant. And when you fell
with a man's child and I was cautious on you
and when you said thisaways and on days
were thataways, I thought your eyes and hair,
of course I did. And of making you soup,
then of making you a bed. And of general solve.
Now, well, I wish you. And miss. Years turn
on such abracadabras. Sleep deeply. Outro.

Plaintive 11

OKR. Our old, shared highway home; a sign
announces 'late night surfacing'. And it is
a lie in some ways to say nothing happened
but notice we do not take turns to thrum
a softly stringed guitar, we do not share
a whispered fantasy of a redhead we would like
between us. See, I have never thumbed down
a page of this book I know you would savour.
I do not sneak the fridge to bring you a treat
with brightest intent, girl, my cadillac resolve.

Plaintive 12

Near mid night and we are seeking Adolphe Sax,
his nationality, his dates, and Sam is busking
the 400 spud alto he is selling. Every one
loves Livi, every one finds the Aussie a waning pesk.
Wobble, since I hear Bella has moved back south.
Next time a gate is shut I hope that the gate
can stay shut. Wobble and not solve. Ambrose
Bierce said of the sax that it was beer's synonym.
People, I knew I could not keep this in the air.
Wobble, and I will grasp tomorrow if I can reach.

Plaintive 13

The divide between sulk and huff invigilated,
a watch kept on simmer and puff, ladies,
men of catchment, I need your deal on this,
we need to solve. A raspy face is never it.
I long to meet you all with super smile.
I have scowled too long and want the planet
to know my sweetheart tendencies. Come on.
War. Other girns have stopped on my watch.
The small girl in *A Special Pleader* kinks
her right heel toward the doting collie.

Plaintive 14

I think you saying read it again, read to me,
and it's complicated. Best, yes, not to write this
for I have lived enough to understand this,
aged and changed by my head. People, I see,
wrap their cars, for reasons. Some know god.
A gap in the twentieth century. Possible.
Pat took me aside and said, we are worried
about you, Roddy. I dream of falling slow
to sleep in the grip of one woman who knows
where I will be when I wake. To be simply that.

Plaintive 15

Girl. About three. Announces that 'the angler fish
lives deep in the midnight zone'. Not reading.
Then she counts to a hundred, aww, ending
27, 28, 29, a hundred. Later, I will watch,
for the hundredth time, the first scene
of *Drowning By Numbers*. I am what I am
at the minute and know the substance. Not been
hugged in a while. Wish I could count not how.
It seems there are people who make computations,
that the world will wrap me when I deserve.

Plaintive 16

Barber loved storms and not the terriers
and little girls it made him nauseous to paint.
My favourite is of course the girl in *Suspense*
who celebrates this year her one hundred
and twentieth birthday, still saying grace,
still about to knock the cap off her egg.
Do I not have wish? Do I shun sentiment?
Days rock past. Even the best of kisses
is improved by hindsight, and by Mozart,
no doubt, though remade till insufferably sad.

Plaintive 17

Do not talk of all the broken things, this
handleless cup, the botched over carpet.
One man's broken side plate is another's
sweetlash memory. All crockery collects
its store of lust and worry. And no need,
here, to hustle this as metaphor. You get it.
You have come this far. Where the bee sucks,
so suck you. And shall I live? Perhaps as broke.
Perhaps remembering too much and gathering
too little new. Sighing beneath scant blossom.

Plaintive 18

The heart asks pleasure first. I seek to solve,
the *little anodynes*, the meeting of eyes,
the way a promise totters on its shy
and must be knocked. I'd meet with you.
We would talk well, I know, as we talk well:
Forteana, psychology, psychpop, verses,
and what is behind the wall. I feel sure
we might mention *that* or our knowsome eyes
would say we both know of behind the wall
and this day we need not mention what is there.

Plaintive 19

My fingerprints are all over this. Can
you tell it is me? Those who are not like me
ought to think hard on why they are not,
though not to dwell, and do not worry,
I will wrap a thoughtful gift, though not too
expensive or neatly wrapped. I have drifted
from the solve. If I am going to die, first
I must make satay, first I must lean against me,
then I must clear from my rattletrap thoughts
the thought that you might recognise or pity me.

Plaintive 20

Wobble. Solve. The major things, such as
they are: Bella dancing to 'Such Great Heights',
Scratch Perry zonking 'Complete Control',
The Stones, feet up at Muscle Shoals, knowing
they have toughed it good. Perry's real name
is Rainford. Still alive, uh, but lying in state
no less. Some die before they die. Some are great
and need no rain, no sun. I do need sun. I need
to say yes to the things which are shaking
their collective heads at me. I weep ambition.

Plaintive 21

The Realms of the Unreal? And Richter spooling.
The Old People of the Little Sisters of the Poor Plot
being the place Darger is buried. Too young, me,
to have met Darger and have got him, and too old
still, now, spooling. No one got. When I was 1973,
war was compact, collectable. I knocked down.
My grandfather fought in a frozen kilt at the Somme,
little chance of running. I stared into Darger's
preserved room for an hour and then went to a bar
and drank beer to prove I have had a simple life.

Plaintive 22

Darger saying novenas for the murdered Elsie.
Barber bumming out another dog and girl thing.
Now me, now me, rubbishing my own night,
seeing off, my heart going in the way it goes.
Partial to the fray. Partial to repeating 'partial'.
Any thing that repeats is fine with me. Give me
a swimming pool I can cross in gentle widths.
Have you ever done any thing twice? Say yes.
I have lived golden, I have lived horrid stony.
I have stunned my loving for doing it wrong.

Plaintive 23

Cherubish, slinking in from the balcony
so much skinnier than I was, no longer
fearing what I so soon ago feared: great stags
which might rut me, the deaths of stars
of minor films, Tyburn, that way the oven
is hot hot. Do you know, my slick compatriots,
what fears you, and how to solve? What, I ask,
is itchy? What bilious? Shall I tell you what
I have been? No, no, too many questions.
A wood still waits that I will walk with her.

Plaintive 24

Walking in, while it still can be called that,
the Victorians still thick in my memory,
seems so. I rush to call the others down now,
by which I mean the others which mean to me.
Romans took to straightest roads, the Hindus
to cow talk. I take to the start and the end
of 'Time It's Time'. Love troubles through me,
often brief, though I wish it were not so.
I think of flat things I could do – reading bad
or maybe the sorting of bedwear or curtains.

Plaintive 25

If I darn for comfort, it will have to be
wool in the belly button or something weighty
I can hide under. Shifts in all industry.
Is it now okay to long for cloth? Okay, R?
Leather, yes, I get it, for others. Sackcloth
does for hermits and other things that Roddy
can never aspire to. Oh, the world. Oh, horror,
the Victorian world. *The Blue Pool at Furzebrook
constantly varies in colour,* some experts say.
And I am expert in my knowing my soft tendency.

Plaintive 26

After the muddy start, the rush of the all bold.
And 1968ness and 1882ness and the dizzy.
The dizzy torque of the late spring weather.
Some people can't *ain't,* some cannot suffer
to say no to a pounding heart. In a suitcase,
I found a soft, black table cloth I did not know
that I owned. I spread it over my refusals.
Warhol never dreamed, but he could say no.
Giotto said no most days to at least one enemy.
Know my art is the very least part of my art.

Plaintive 27

Beaufort mazing the rain, a Cro-Magnon.
Degas, eyes on the small girl defying
the pianoforte, an unidentified hominid.
Greenaway, in his cave with, I guess,
some sort of head wound, philosophising
the shadows from the fire. The only woman
who has ever turned my dom thoughts to sub
will never seesaw me over her shoulder
and thump me onto the ashes, hers in absolute.
So seldom we deserve what we have wanted.

Plaintive 28

Do not try and explain some thing to any one,
the plot of *Ponette* say, or mah jong rules.
The young have it easier, they do not yet
have that yearning dread and do not fall easy.
Rope rarely interests me. Thread, I can go
a whole day without pothering on. We only have
one inhabitable world and it is an insatiable pesk.
Rules make ruins. Explication eeks ruin's edges.
Some have claimed that Christ had all the passion
but believe me, babies, I have all the passion.

Plaintive 29

I want a red sweater like Ponette's. And to talk
to the wall and for the wall to be my bestie.
I got God only briefly and then saw that things
had a handle, that things tended to anchorage
and that God was not that capable a character.
Darger loved God, Barber went to him soon.
I mildly like the life I found. Which I was given.
My parents met at a dance. I have never even been
to a dance. Tonight I am wearing my father's shirt.
I am wearing my mother and father, as you can tell.

Plaintive 30

Today is cancelled due to lack of interest,
says Raina, again, straddling me. A catchphrase
from her dead partner. She is swivelling
between kissing me and crying. Awkward. Adele
at the Albert Hall is playing on a televised loop.
A loop. *And not a child washed in the house.*
We keep apologising to one another. The walk
home across the heath has me whistling, but
it's that Nyman piece where Madgett sinks
at the dim of things. Some doom days are partial.

Plaintive 31

The moon is always falling. My new shoes
are speckled with grass seed. And the son
you had early slept somewhere near us;
he's the same age as my last three lovers.
Driven by the white wine you call 'lady petrol',
you chimed, *let's be, let's be, let's be, let's be*.
Night ducks on the *Princess* pond. That weave
of worriment and uplift that follows kisses
draws me home. *One thought waits with you now*.
The blooded dark, that the night sheens through it.

Plaintive 32

So soon the recent becomes the plaintive present:
Bella jigging to 'Once and for All'. You may think
you think twice, but mice and the fousty smells
of books duff my life. I was thinking pertly of
the longest walk I have ever done. Sorry, no idea.
James asked me the weirdest thing any woman
had ever asked me to do to her, and now I see.
I do not wish a long walk thank you, I am human.
Pillow queens, worriers, self-haters, love was what
I tried and some times, in my dizzy way, did to you.

Plaintive 33

Damn and now I dream of pillow queening her:
'no response kissing' then 'breath sucking' then
'extreme kissing' then 'full body kiss'. Relax, girl,
except don't. Well, I'd decide that for you. Weather
today is what as a child I named 'a plain day'.
Someone is listening to the shipping forecast,
not truly getting it, someone checks a rain gauge,
another looks at clouds then looks up which type.
I have changed the subject haven't I? You know
now what I am though I feel you guessed before.

Plaintive 34

Never abseiled. Never been Saxon. Never
seen tundra. Never crossed the equator, yet.
Never been mistaken for a wine waiter.
Never eaten bison. Never sang a madrigal,
yet. Never been kept awake by rutting dogs
and never counted to more than a hundred,
aloud I mean. Never visited Crete, or happiness.
Never operated a lathe in a professional sense.
Never sailed a river. Never solved, yet. Never
missed you, yet. Never needed you. Never lied.

Plaintive 35

Everything's gone Greenaway. You trance
that the intimacy has gone, though business,
the fleshy business survives. A wrong name
sylphs and your time jinks. My parents
and my brothers married young. That was not
open to me. I jilt and am jilted and dabble.
World counts a hundred. World says sorry.
Sorry. The lights turn quirky and I am Roddy.
Fire in the caves. I wrestle myself home.
I deserve to watch wrestling, only now I realise.

Plaintive 36

Sarah, I knew you would push your head into this.
Temptation is the least of it. I am stronger
than it. How is Leeds? Maybe, what is Leeds?
Who of my grandparents were true Victorians?
One. Victoria looted her own sad lootings
and died old though history would prefer
if she had gone younger. You and I were
best not say. All love is consumption, gas.
I strike along some alley and think, hey,
I am someone, but I am far off someone.

Plaintive 37

Victoria not going to a hanging. Solve.
Victoria needing. Bonnie girl. Victoria
rushing to an exit. Victoria losing things,
easy things, like Raina with her keys.
Solve. Meadow queen with a taste
for the everafter, who did not believe
girls kiss girls. Girls kiss girls. Tight
is a word that edgies me, tight, you know.
I worry about tight but I worry anyhow;
worry is the friend who walks with me.

Plaintive 38

Small boy, you know, local and acting up
and his Mum points outs a picture
of a 'shark'. It's a fish on the chip shop
window but he calms. Did you ever calm?
Solve. My head changed when my head
got hit. Solve. Sharks never love me,
people, I tried. Combine harvesters
were my effusion. Yeah, I dwelt on things,
was loving. Calm? I know it like I know
the back of the beyond of the beyond.

Plaintive 39

Nyman's 'Time Lapse' drives the way
I walk now. Some people have said some
blistering things about the past. Solve.
Solve. *Wrap the starry plough around me*.
I aim to be the one who may test your dreams.
Who lived in dangerous days? All, all.
Who... oh, I have done enough who in this life.
In the next life, I promise, I will never ask who.
Time lapses. *The matador, raving*. Icy stings
will staunch my last, my last few breaths.

Plaintive 40

I would not have liked Darger, pity mostly.
Pity I would have discussed with Barber,
not mentioning the girls or dogs. The rush,
do you know what I mean by the rush,
do I have to explain that? I fell again.
My conspiracy is my own conspiracy.
Ice hockey players grow piratical beards
as the season passes. My stoury, vinegary
beard grows as I sing myself through this,
gibbonish, the canopy hissing above me.

Plaintive 41

Monkey boy. Caveman. Sitter. Aristo
of the minor. Reduced courage. Wobble.
Solve. Heya Catherine Cookson, heya
singers of rebel songs. Some nights just
do not last long enough. If, say, Prospero
is just as real as people I have kissed,
will things tumble? Both Unthinkable
and Luscious things have happened to me.
Dimster. Non-acrobat. Shyster. Faffer.
Rabbit of my own dim warren, cowering.

Plaintive 42

Mozart, Cookson, Love. I choose Love.
With a capital. I'd build the capital.
Am I the only person to reflect (reflect?)
on walks I have taken with others? Bella
on the Heath. With James down to Greenwich.
My Dad taking us to the Rock and Spindle.
The Devil's Frying Pan, where I bottled
and tried to walk, walk meaning walk away.
Most of all I hate the word *away*. I wish
away did not scout me. Do not scout me.

Plaintive 43

Best thing in a world, aye ayes of course,
then I could name some women I have loved
but that would annoy you. Being busy hurts.
I prefer the love really. Love came hurdling
when I was boy. I saw its face and it scared
the face off me. I needed to count the wrong
of things and I am not pure O, just maybe Aspy.
I can count to a hundred, just ask. The smell
of aye ayes does not put me off. They stink
but love stinks and love is all I have, folks.

Plaintive 44

The minor knights of the Round Table
are circling. The woman in *The Last of England*
is so like a sun, astronomers are twitching
their focuses. Alex comes home from the office
in the mood for some twang. Candy dithers
in glass jars, all the dayglo shades. Kate, tipsy,
sings me Ivor Novello. Amanda sighs and says
okay, just one more jag of processed cheese.
Nutella hangs in its bottle, *a spoonful weighs a ton*,
getting heavy heavy. Gravity pulls its weight.

Plaintive 45

Mariachi flourishes, you think I don't get them?
The vase of irises you place above my senses?
Highwayman stories, or double acrostics
left by my yellowy pillow. I am on to you.
Hand me a Malibu, I'll roll my eyes, but, but
don't expect me to break. I am system one.
I am the start of 'New Dawn Fades'. Expect me
to keel in some way soon, tried by your kitsch.
But I will keel and solve. I grew by the sea.
Never think you can drag me from that sea.

Plaintive 46

Tiens? 'Really' or 'hold' or 'yours' or 'look'.
Hold, solve. Come with me to this corner?
Camellia prefers an old style to the new.
I am not right sure yet which style I am.
But 'hold' will do me. My French is weak,
even though my name and history is French.
No one knows who invented candy, or law,
or dynamite, but some continue to hold
through nights which would otherwise
be hopeless. No trust if you think different.

Plaintive 47

Oh, now I want to throw Romeo and Juliet
into *The Tempest*. At this uncommon moment,
nothing would be more. How they would be
rained upon and seek the edges of an island.
A storm would blue them and I could jump up.
Did I say would? No one, admit it, likes Prospero.
or the voices of certain singers who make me
cry late at night. Islands, I see, are secondary
to our tears. We collect, not break. Uneven love
has made me cry, but you know that, everywhere.

Plaintive 48

Help me, I am listening to 'He'll Have To Go'
and looking at old photographs of Bella.
All emotional risk is busking at my ear.
Do not tell me you have not been in this box.
I wonder if Darger was night or morning.
If I look at parrots, perhaps parrots will aid me.
I'm sure I never went to Hopechapel Hill.
Solve is off. I miss the girl, is it okay to?
I do not need big chat. I need harmonica.
That and the girl not running, running away.

Plaintive 49

Village is as Village does and sorts. Solves?
Solve. Barber painted the small girls first
and then the dogs. Raina sings 'Moon River',
the whole song, close to my ear. That doesn't
happen too often in a natural life. Her fist-sized
ginger kitten jumps, not yet at hunting. Or hurt.
What Capote lost, the ether gained, it seems.
I am always two oar lengths from chaotic
but when a woman sings at my ear, I can, -ish,
tideway the direction from which I was brought.

Plaintive 50

Mozart. If I did meet Greenaway I would explain
that ringlety, plump brunettes are all I need
but that I could never admit that in a poem.
Never. In 'Porphyria's Lover', as in this one,
it is the man who dies, or have I remembered that
wrong? Solve. Some lie at night thinking Samson,
or Samson. Night has shifted me. Brusk night,
a crumbled biscuit. The barber weaves toward me,
his scissors itching. What I have done I have done
not for dulce or decorum, but for the et, and the est.

Notes

long term concussion in midwinter (midlife) – a mistigris is a joker used as a wild card in certain forms of poker

rain on tranquil vale (rem sleep) – the railway is the name of a pub on Tranquil Vale, S London; the skin of the honey badger is very loose, allowing it to escape aggressive situations; the honeyguide is a bird which leads mammals to beehives, later clearing up the spoils

late night conversation (brian) – it has been suggested that some of Henry VIII's marriages went awry due to a pungent smell caused by a wound which never properly healed; Henry first properly met Anne of Cleves at Blackheath in January 1540; they were disappointed by each other's looks and the marriage was destined not to work

the thames at limehouse (∴ wide) – microsaccades are tiny, involuntary eye movements which happen when we are focussing on something we are concentrating on; this poem springs from a situation in which myself and three poet friends were challenged to do impressions of one another

late night conversation (frith) – this poem alludes to the song 'The Lonesome Death of Hattie Carroll' by Bob Dylan

rain on tranquil vale (retro) – Kasenetz and Katz were US record producers who are credited with creating the 'bubblegum pop' genre in the late 1960s; 'sugar shoppe' is a reference to the innuendo-laden track 'Candy' recorded by the young stars of hit show *The Brady Bunch*

long term concussion in midwinter (mid evening) – 'Fractions' is a song by the Australian group Decoder Ring

late night conversation (josh) – lie detectors are thought to be far more effective in crimes of passion than in the conviction of hardened criminals

late night conversation (dominic) – 'music of the primes' is a term sometimes used by mathematicians for the unfathom-able patterning of prime numbers

late night conversation (heidi) – Taupin as in Bernie Taupin, long term lyricist for Elton John whose songs have often explored stereotypes of Americana

late night conversation (frith) – the homes of Frida Kahlo and Diego Rivera were separated by a bridge

long term concussion in spring (establishing) – the foodstuffs mentioned here are all traditional dishes served at weddings

rain on tranquil vale (res gestae) – 'res gestae' means 'what is done'; Gavrilo Princip, who shot Franz Ferdinand, had apparently given up on his assassination plan until the car happened to take a wrong turning and passed where he was walking

long term concussion in spring (esurient) – a namtap is an exotic breed of dormouse and is my nickname for a friend of mine

rain on tranquil vale (reggae) – 'greek it up' is an entertainment term for making a film or show more dramatic; 'Peeni Walli' is a song by the reggae singer Eek-A-Mouse about a bicycle accident; peeni walli are tiny insects, used in this song as an idiom similar to 'seeing stars' after a head knock

late night conversation (jesus and the crusader) – nicknames for two local friends

rain on tranquil vale (reward) – 'Rainy Night in Soho' is a song by The Pogues; the fox was kept at a local abattoir so its scent would keep away other foxes; it was the nearest thing to a zoo during my childhood

long term concussion in early summer (suture) – references here to Tori Amos' break-up album *Boys for Pele* and the late life of the poet WS Graham in Cornwall; the names in the final couplet are all names of potential daughters from discussions in past relationships

Plaintive 20 – there is a reference here to a film clip of The Rolling Stones, having just finished the recording of the song 'Wild Horses'

Plaintive 21 – The full name of Darger's gigantic novel was *The Story of the Vivian Girls, in What is Known as the Realms of the Unreal, of the Glandeco-Angelinian War Storm, Caused by the Child Slave Rebellion*

Plaintive 28 – *Ponette* is a bleak but beautiful French film from 1996 which is based around a four year old girl trying to understand the death of her mother. Many of its scenes are improvised by very young child actors

Plaintive 30 – Madgett is the main character in *Drowning by Numbers*

Plaintive 32 – a pillow queen is a woman who wants to be or agrees to be the centre of intimate attention

Plaintive 43 – 'pure O' is a form of OCD where the person has strong obsessions but no compulsions

Plaintive 48 – 'big chat' is a shorthand term for 'introspective relationship talk'

Playlist

Young Marble Giants – 'N.I.T.A.'
Bob Dylan – 'The Lonesome Death of Hattie Carroll'
Decoder Ring – 'Fractions'
Elton John – 'Crocodile Rock'
Emmylou Harris – 'Here, There and Everywhere'
Fleetwood Mac - 'I Know I'm Not Wrong'
Eek-A-Mouse – 'Peeni Walli'
The Pogues – 'Rainy Night in Soho'
Tori Amos – 'Horses'
Microdisney – '464'
Michael Nyman – 'Big My Secret'
Harold Budd – 'Children on the Hill'
Drop Nineteens – 'Winona'
The Postal Service – 'Such Great Heights'
The Clash – 'Complete Control'
The Rolling Stones – 'Wild Horses'
Max Richter - 'On the Nature of Daylight'
Talk Talk – 'Time It's Time'
Clock Opera – 'Once and for All'
Dominant Legs – 'Calm Down'
New Order – 'Everything's Gone Green'
Michael Nyman – 'Time Lapse'
Christy Moore – 'The Contender'
Flaming Lips – 'A Spoonful Weighs a Ton'
Joy Division – 'New Dawn Fades'
Jim Reeves – 'He'll Have to Go'
Gravenhurst – 'Hopechapel Hill'
Audrey Hepburn – 'Moon River'

Also available from Salt

ELIZABETH BAINES
Too Many Magpies (978-1-84471-721-7)
The Birth Machine (978-1-907773-02-0)

LESLEY GLAISTER
Little Egypt (978-1-907773-72-3)

ALISON MOORE
The Lighthouse (978-1-907773-17-4)
The PreWar House and Other Stories (978-1-907773-50-1)
He Wants (978-1-907773815)

ALICE THOMPSON
Justine (978-1-78463-032-4)
The Falconer (978-1-78463-009-6)
The Existential Detective (978-1-78463-011-9)
Burnt Island (978-1-907773-48-8)

MEIKE ZIERVOGEL
Magda (978-1-907773-40-2)
Clara's Daughter (978-1-907773-79-2)
Kauthar (978-1-78463-029-4)

Next Generation poets at Salt

TOBIAS HILL
Year of the Dog (978-1-84471-553-4)
Midnight in the City of Clocks (978-1-84471-549-7)
Zoo (978-1-84471-413-1)
Nocturne in Chrome & Sunset Yellow (1844712621)

LUKE KENNARD
The Solex Brothers (Redux) (978-1-844715-48-0)
The Harbour Beyond the Movie (978-1-84471-533-6)
The Migraine Hotel (978-1-84471-555-8)
A Lost Expression (978-1-84471-875-7)

MARK WALDRON
The Brand New Dark (978-1-84471-817-7)
The Itchy Sea (978-1-84471-827-6)

Also available from Salt

New fiction from Salt